50 Whole Grain Bread Recipes for Home

By: Kelly Johnson

Table of Contents

- Whole Wheat Sandwich Bread
- Multigrain Seeded Loaf
- Honey Oat Bread
- Spelt and Flaxseed Bread
- Quinoa and Sunflower Seed Bread
- Rye and Caraway Bread
- Buckwheat and Chia Seed Loaf
- Teff and Millet Bread
- Barley and Walnut Bread
- Amaranth and Pumpkin Seed Bread
- Brown Rice Flour Bread
- Bulgur and Pecan Loaf
- Kamut and Sesame Seed Bread
- Einkorn and Poppy Seed Bread
- Farro and Hazelnut Bread
- Millet and Cranberry Bread
- Emmer and Almond Loaf
- Sorghum and Pine Nut Bread
- Whole Spelt Bagels
- Sunflower Seed Rye Rolls
- Whole Wheat Sourdough Boule
- Flax and Chia Swirl Bread
- Three-Seed Whole Grain Flatbread
- Oat Bran and Date Loaf
- Ancient Grains Ciabatta
- Muesli Bread with Dried Fruit
- Quinoa and Amaranth Focaccia
- Sun-Dried Tomato and Basil Spelt Bread
- Buckwheat and Almond Biscuits
- Walnut and Fig Whole Grain Bread
- Pumpkin Seed Rye Sourdough
- Millet and Blueberry Breakfast Bread
- Whole Wheat Pita Bread
- Barley and Olive Loaf
- 7-Grain Dinner Rolls

- Hazelnut and Date Spelt Bread
- Sweet Potato and Quinoa Bread
- Einkorn and Raisin Baguettes
- Walnut and Cranberry Multigrain Bread
- Spelt and Rosemary Fougasse
- Oat and Apricot Breadsticks
- Kamut and Date Nut Rolls
- Millet and Sunflower Seed Bagels
- Quinoa and Cranberry Swirl Bread
- Whole Wheat Pizza Dough
- Buckwheat and Fig Sourdough
- Pumpkin Seed and Apricot Loaf
- Teff and Date Flatbread
- Amaranth and Currant Bread
- Sunflower Seed and Honey Rye Bread

Whole Wheat Sandwich Bread

Ingredients:

- 3 cups whole wheat flour
- 1 ½ teaspoons active dry yeast
- 1 ½ cups warm water (about 110°F/43°C)
- 2 tablespoons honey or maple syrup
- 2 tablespoons olive oil
- 1 teaspoon salt

Instructions:

In a small bowl, combine the warm water and honey. Sprinkle the yeast over the water and let it sit for about 5 minutes until it becomes frothy.
In a large mixing bowl, combine the whole wheat flour and salt.
Make a well in the center of the flour mixture and pour in the activated yeast mixture and olive oil.
Mix the ingredients until a dough forms. Knead the dough on a floured surface for about 8-10 minutes or until it becomes smooth and elastic.
Place the dough in a lightly oiled bowl, cover it with a damp cloth, and let it rise in a warm place for 1-1.5 hours or until it doubles in size.
Preheat your oven to 375°F (190°C).
Punch down the risen dough and transfer it to a lightly floured surface. Shape it into a loaf.
Place the shaped dough into a greased loaf pan. Cover it with a cloth and let it rise for another 30-45 minutes.
Bake in the preheated oven for 25-30 minutes or until the bread sounds hollow when tapped on the bottom.
Remove the bread from the oven and let it cool in the pan for 10 minutes before transferring it to a wire rack to cool completely.
Once the bread has cooled, slice it and enjoy for sandwiches or toast!

Feel free to adjust the sweetness, add seeds, or incorporate a mix of whole grains to customize the recipe to your liking.

Multigrain Seeded Loaf

Ingredients:

- 1 ½ cups warm water (about 110°F/43°C)
- 2 teaspoons active dry yeast
- 2 tablespoons honey or maple syrup
- 1 cup whole wheat flour
- 1 cup bread flour
- ½ cup rolled oats
- ¼ cup flaxseeds
- ¼ cup sunflower seeds
- ¼ cup sesame seeds
- 2 tablespoons chia seeds
- 2 tablespoons pumpkin seeds
- 2 tablespoons olive oil
- 1 teaspoon salt

Instructions:

In a small bowl, combine the warm water and honey. Sprinkle the yeast over the water and let it sit for about 5 minutes until it becomes frothy.

In a large mixing bowl, combine the whole wheat flour, bread flour, rolled oats, flaxseeds, sunflower seeds, sesame seeds, chia seeds, and pumpkin seeds.

Make a well in the center of the flour mixture and pour in the activated yeast mixture and olive oil.

Mix the ingredients until a dough forms. Knead the dough on a floured surface for about 8-10 minutes or until it becomes smooth and elastic.

Place the dough in a lightly oiled bowl, cover it with a damp cloth, and let it rise in a warm place for 1-1.5 hours or until it doubles in size.

Preheat your oven to 375°F (190°C).

Punch down the risen dough and transfer it to a lightly floured surface. Shape it into a loaf.

In a small bowl, mix together a tablespoon of water and a tablespoon of seeds (sesame, flax, sunflower, etc.). Brush the top of the loaf with this mixture to help the seeds adhere.

Place the shaped dough into a greased loaf pan. Cover it with a cloth and let it rise for another 30-45 minutes.

Bake in the preheated oven for 30-35 minutes or until the bread sounds hollow when tapped on the bottom.

Remove the bread from the oven and let it cool in the pan for 10 minutes before transferring it to a wire rack to cool completely.

Once the bread has cooled, slice it and enjoy the nutty, seedy goodness!

Feel free to customize the seed mix based on your preferences, and you can add additional grains or seeds for more variety and texture.

Honey Oat Bread

Ingredients:

- 1 cup old-fashioned oats
- 1 ½ cups boiling water
- 2 tablespoons unsalted butter
- ¼ cup honey
- 2 ¼ teaspoons active dry yeast
- 1 ½ teaspoons salt
- 4 to 4 ½ cups bread flour

Instructions:

In a large bowl, combine the oats, boiling water, butter, and honey. Stir well and let it sit for about 15-20 minutes, or until the mixture has cooled to lukewarm.
Sprinkle the yeast over the oat mixture and let it sit for 5 minutes until it becomes frothy.
Add the salt and start adding the bread flour, one cup at a time, mixing well after each addition. Continue adding flour until the dough begins to pull away from the sides of the bowl.
Turn the dough out onto a floured surface and knead for about 8-10 minutes until it becomes smooth and elastic. Add more flour as needed to prevent sticking.
Place the dough in a lightly oiled bowl, cover it with a damp cloth, and let it rise in a warm place for 1-1.5 hours or until it doubles in size.
Preheat your oven to 375°F (190°C).
Punch down the risen dough and transfer it to a lightly floured surface. Shape it into a loaf.
Place the shaped dough into a greased loaf pan. Cover it with a cloth and let it rise for another 30-45 minutes.
Bake in the preheated oven for 30-35 minutes or until the bread sounds hollow when tapped on the bottom.
In the last 10 minutes of baking, you can brush the top of the loaf with a little melted butter for a shiny finish.
Remove the bread from the oven and let it cool in the pan for 10 minutes before transferring it to a wire rack to cool completely.
Once the bread has cooled, slice it and enjoy the delicious honey-infused oat bread!

This honey oat bread is perfect for sandwiches or toasting, and the oats give it a wonderful texture. Adjust the honey amount based on your sweetness preference.

Spelt and Flaxseed Bread

Ingredients:

- 1 ½ cups warm water (about 110°F/43°C)
- 2 teaspoons active dry yeast
- 1 tablespoon honey or maple syrup
- 3 cups spelt flour
- 1 cup bread flour
- ¼ cup ground flaxseeds
- 2 tablespoons whole flaxseeds (for topping)
- 2 tablespoons olive oil
- 1 teaspoon salt

Instructions:

In a small bowl, combine the warm water and honey. Sprinkle the yeast over the water and let it sit for about 5 minutes until it becomes frothy.

In a large mixing bowl, combine the spelt flour, bread flour, and ground flaxseeds. Make a well in the center of the flour mixture and pour in the activated yeast mixture and olive oil.

Mix the ingredients until a dough forms. Knead the dough on a floured surface for about 8-10 minutes or until it becomes smooth and elastic.

Place the dough in a lightly oiled bowl, cover it with a damp cloth, and let it rise in a warm place for 1-1.5 hours or until it doubles in size.

Preheat your oven to 375°F (190°C).

Punch down the risen dough and transfer it to a lightly floured surface. Shape it into a loaf.

Place the shaped dough into a greased loaf pan. Brush the top with water and sprinkle whole flaxseeds over it for a decorative touch.

Cover it with a cloth and let it rise for another 30-45 minutes.

Bake in the preheated oven for 30-35 minutes or until the bread sounds hollow when tapped on the bottom.

Remove the bread from the oven and let it cool in the pan for 10 minutes before transferring it to a wire rack to cool completely.

Once the bread has cooled, slice it and enjoy the wholesome goodness of spelt and flaxseed!

Feel free to experiment by adding other seeds or nuts for extra texture and flavor. This bread is a nutritious option with the nutty taste of spelt and the health benefits of flaxseeds.

Quinoa and Sunflower Seed Bread

Ingredients:

- 1 cup cooked quinoa, cooled
- 1 ½ cups warm water (about 110°F/43°C)
- 2 teaspoons active dry yeast
- 1 tablespoon honey or maple syrup
- 3 cups bread flour
- 1 cup whole wheat flour
- ½ cup sunflower seeds (plus extra for topping)
- 2 tablespoons olive oil
- 1 teaspoon salt

Instructions:

In a small bowl, combine the warm water and honey. Sprinkle the yeast over the water and let it sit for about 5 minutes until it becomes frothy.

In a large mixing bowl, combine the bread flour, whole wheat flour, and sunflower seeds.

In another bowl, mix the cooked quinoa and olive oil.

Make a well in the center of the flour mixture and pour in the activated yeast mixture and the quinoa mixture.

Mix the ingredients until a dough forms. Knead the dough on a floured surface for about 8-10 minutes or until it becomes smooth and elastic.

Place the dough in a lightly oiled bowl, cover it with a damp cloth, and let it rise in a warm place for 1-1.5 hours or until it doubles in size.

Preheat your oven to 375°F (190°C).

Punch down the risen dough and transfer it to a lightly floured surface. Shape it into a loaf.

Place the shaped dough into a greased loaf pan. Brush the top with water and sprinkle additional sunflower seeds over it for added crunch and visual appeal.

Cover it with a cloth and let it rise for another 30-45 minutes.

Bake in the preheated oven for 30-35 minutes or until the bread sounds hollow when tapped on the bottom.

Remove the bread from the oven and let it cool in the pan for 10 minutes before transferring it to a wire rack to cool completely.

Once the bread has cooled, slice it and enjoy the nutty flavor and texture of quinoa and sunflower seeds!

This quinoa and sunflower seed bread is a hearty, protein-rich option with a delightful crunch from the sunflower seeds. Adjust the honey amount based on your sweetness preference.

Rye and Caraway Bread

Ingredients:

- 1 ½ cups warm water (about 110°F/43°C)
- 2 teaspoons active dry yeast
- 1 tablespoon honey or molasses
- 1 cup rye flour
- 2 ½ cups bread flour
- 2 tablespoons caraway seeds (plus extra for topping)
- 2 tablespoons olive oil
- 1 teaspoon salt

Instructions:

In a small bowl, combine the warm water and honey. Sprinkle the yeast over the water and let it sit for about 5 minutes until it becomes frothy.

In a large mixing bowl, combine the rye flour, bread flour, and caraway seeds.

Make a well in the center of the flour mixture and pour in the activated yeast mixture and olive oil.

Mix the ingredients until a dough forms. Knead the dough on a floured surface for about 8-10 minutes or until it becomes smooth and elastic.

Place the dough in a lightly oiled bowl, cover it with a damp cloth, and let it rise in a warm place for 1-1.5 hours or until it doubles in size.

Preheat your oven to 375°F (190°C).

Punch down the risen dough and transfer it to a lightly floured surface. Shape it into a round or oval loaf.

Place the shaped dough onto a baking sheet lined with parchment paper. Brush the top with water and sprinkle additional caraway seeds over it for flavor and decoration.

Cover it with a cloth and let it rise for another 30-45 minutes.

Bake in the preheated oven for 30-35 minutes or until the bread sounds hollow when tapped on the bottom.

Remove the bread from the oven and let it cool on a wire rack.

Once the bread has cooled, slice it and enjoy the distinctive flavor of rye and caraway!

This rye and caraway bread is perfect for sandwiches, especially with classic pairings like pastrami and mustard. Adjust the honey or molasses amount based on your desired level of sweetness.

Buckwheat and Chia Seed Loaf

Ingredients:

- 1 ½ cups warm water (about 110°F/43°C)
- 2 teaspoons active dry yeast
- 1 tablespoon honey or maple syrup
- 2 cups buckwheat flour
- 1 cup all-purpose flour
- ¼ cup chia seeds
- 2 tablespoons olive oil
- 1 teaspoon salt

Instructions:

In a small bowl, combine the warm water and honey. Sprinkle the yeast over the water and let it sit for about 5 minutes until it becomes frothy.

In a large mixing bowl, combine the buckwheat flour, all-purpose flour, and chia seeds.

Make a well in the center of the flour mixture and pour in the activated yeast mixture and olive oil.

Mix the ingredients until a dough forms. Knead the dough on a floured surface for about 8-10 minutes or until it becomes smooth and elastic.

Place the dough in a lightly oiled bowl, cover it with a damp cloth, and let it rise in a warm place for 1-1.5 hours or until it doubles in size.

Preheat your oven to 375°F (190°C).

Punch down the risen dough and transfer it to a lightly floured surface. Shape it into a loaf.

Place the shaped dough into a greased loaf pan. Cover it with a cloth and let it rise for another 30-45 minutes.

Bake in the preheated oven for 30-35 minutes or until the bread sounds hollow when tapped on the bottom.

Remove the bread from the oven and let it cool in the pan for 10 minutes before transferring it to a wire rack to cool completely.

Once the bread has cooled, slice it and enjoy the nutty flavor and crunch from the buckwheat and chia seeds!

This buckwheat and chia seed loaf is not only delicious but also packed with nutritional benefits. Adjust the honey or maple syrup amount based on your sweetness preference.

Teff and Millet Bread

Ingredients:

- 1 ½ cups warm water (about 110°F/43°C)
- 2 teaspoons active dry yeast
- 1 tablespoon honey or agave syrup
- 2 cups teff flour
- 1 cup millet flour
- 1 cup all-purpose flour
- 2 tablespoons olive oil
- 1 teaspoon salt
- Additional millet seeds for topping (optional)

Instructions:

In a small bowl, combine the warm water and honey. Sprinkle the yeast over the water and let it sit for about 5 minutes until it becomes frothy.
In a large mixing bowl, combine the teff flour, millet flour, all-purpose flour, and salt.
Make a well in the center of the flour mixture and pour in the activated yeast mixture and olive oil.
Mix the ingredients until a dough forms. Knead the dough on a floured surface for about 8-10 minutes or until it becomes smooth and elastic.
Place the dough in a lightly oiled bowl, cover it with a damp cloth, and let it rise in a warm place for 1-1.5 hours or until it doubles in size.
Preheat your oven to 375°F (190°C).
Punch down the risen dough and transfer it to a lightly floured surface. Shape it into a loaf.
Place the shaped dough into a greased loaf pan. If desired, brush the top with water and sprinkle additional millet seeds for extra texture.
Cover it with a cloth and let it rise for another 30-45 minutes.
Bake in the preheated oven for 30-35 minutes or until the bread sounds hollow when tapped on the bottom.
Remove the bread from the oven and let it cool in the pan for 10 minutes before transferring it to a wire rack to cool completely.
Once the bread has cooled, slice it and enjoy the unique flavors and textures of teff and millet!

This teff and millet bread is gluten-free and has a rich, nutty flavor. Adjust the honey or agave syrup amount based on your preferred level of sweetness.

Barley and Walnut Bread

Ingredients:

- 1 ½ cups warm water (about 110°F/43°C)
- 2 teaspoons active dry yeast
- 1 tablespoon honey or molasses
- 2 cups barley flour
- 1 cup whole wheat flour
- 1 cup all-purpose flour
- 1 cup chopped walnuts
- 2 tablespoons olive oil
- 1 teaspoon salt

Instructions:

In a small bowl, combine the warm water and honey. Sprinkle the yeast over the water and let it sit for about 5 minutes until it becomes frothy.
In a large mixing bowl, combine the barley flour, whole wheat flour, all-purpose flour, and salt.
Make a well in the center of the flour mixture and pour in the activated yeast mixture and olive oil.
Mix the ingredients until a dough forms. Knead the dough on a floured surface for about 8-10 minutes or until it becomes smooth and elastic.
Fold in the chopped walnuts during the last couple of minutes of kneading to evenly distribute them throughout the dough.
Place the dough in a lightly oiled bowl, cover it with a damp cloth, and let it rise in a warm place for 1-1.5 hours or until it doubles in size.
Preheat your oven to 375°F (190°C).
Punch down the risen dough and transfer it to a lightly floured surface. Shape it into a loaf.
Place the shaped dough into a greased loaf pan. Cover it with a cloth and let it rise for another 30-45 minutes.
Bake in the preheated oven for 30-35 minutes or until the bread sounds hollow when tapped on the bottom.
Remove the bread from the oven and let it cool in the pan for 10 minutes before transferring it to a wire rack to cool completely.
Once the bread has cooled, slice it and enjoy the hearty combination of barley and walnuts!

This barley and walnut bread is not only delicious but also provides a satisfying crunch from the walnuts. Adjust the honey or molasses amount based on your desired level of sweetness.

Amaranth and Pumpkin Seed Bread

Ingredients:

- 1 ½ cups warm water (about 110°F/43°C)
- 2 teaspoons active dry yeast
- 1 tablespoon honey or agave syrup
- 2 cups amaranth flour
- 1 cup whole wheat flour
- 1 cup all-purpose flour
- ½ cup raw pumpkin seeds (plus extra for topping)
- 2 tablespoons olive oil
- 1 teaspoon salt

Instructions:

In a small bowl, combine the warm water and honey. Sprinkle the yeast over the water and let it sit for about 5 minutes until it becomes frothy.

In a large mixing bowl, combine the amaranth flour, whole wheat flour, all-purpose flour, and salt.

Make a well in the center of the flour mixture and pour in the activated yeast mixture and olive oil.

Mix the ingredients until a dough forms. Knead the dough on a floured surface for about 8-10 minutes or until it becomes smooth and elastic.

Fold in the pumpkin seeds during the last couple of minutes of kneading to evenly distribute them throughout the dough.

Place the dough in a lightly oiled bowl, cover it with a damp cloth, and let it rise in a warm place for 1-1.5 hours or until it doubles in size.

Preheat your oven to 375°F (190°C).

Punch down the risen dough and transfer it to a lightly floured surface. Shape it into a loaf.

Place the shaped dough into a greased loaf pan. Brush the top with water and sprinkle additional pumpkin seeds over it for added texture.

Cover it with a cloth and let it rise for another 30-45 minutes.

Bake in the preheated oven for 30-35 minutes or until the bread sounds hollow when tapped on the bottom.

Remove the bread from the oven and let it cool in the pan for 10 minutes before transferring it to a wire rack to cool completely.

Once the bread has cooled, slice it and enjoy the nutty flavor and crunch from the amaranth and pumpkin seeds!

This amaranth and pumpkin seed bread is a wholesome option with a unique combination of flavors and textures. Adjust the honey or agave syrup amount based on your sweetness preference.

Brown Rice Flour Bread

Ingredients:

- 2 cups brown rice flour
- 1 cup tapioca flour
- 1/2 cup potato starch
- 1 tablespoon xanthan gum
- 1 teaspoon salt
- 1 tablespoon active dry yeast
- 1 1/2 cups warm water (around 110°F or 43°C)
- 2 tablespoons honey or maple syrup
- 3 large eggs
- 1/4 cup olive oil or melted coconut oil
- Sesame seeds or other seeds for topping (optional)

Instructions:

Activate Yeast:
- In a small bowl, combine the warm water and honey (or maple syrup).
- Sprinkle the yeast over the water and let it sit for about 5-10 minutes until it becomes frothy.

Mix Dry Ingredients:
- In a large mixing bowl, whisk together the brown rice flour, tapioca flour, potato starch, xanthan gum, and salt.

Combine Wet Ingredients:
- In another bowl, beat the eggs and add the olive oil or melted coconut oil.
- Pour in the activated yeast mixture and mix well.

Combine Wet and Dry Mixtures:
- Add the wet ingredients to the dry ingredients and mix until well combined. The batter will be thick.

Rise Time:
- Transfer the batter into a greased and floured bread pan.
- Cover the pan with a clean kitchen towel and let it rise in a warm place for about 45-60 minutes, or until it doubles in size.

Preheat Oven:
- Preheat your oven to 375°F (190°C).

Bake:
- Optionally, sprinkle sesame seeds or other seeds on top of the risen bread.

- Bake in the preheated oven for 40-45 minutes or until the bread is golden brown and sounds hollow when tapped.

Cool:
- Allow the bread to cool in the pan for about 10 minutes, then transfer it to a wire rack to cool completely before slicing.

Enjoy your homemade brown rice flour bread! You can customize this recipe by adding herbs, seeds, or other flavorings to suit your taste preferences.

Bulgur and Pecan Loaf

Ingredients:

- 1 cup coarse bulgur
- 1 1/2 cups boiling water
- 1 cup finely chopped pecans
- 3 cups bread flour
- 1 packet (2 1/4 teaspoons) active dry yeast
- 1 1/2 teaspoons salt
- 1 tablespoon honey or maple syrup
- 1 cup warm water (around 110°F or 43°C)
- 2 tablespoons olive oil
- 1 egg for egg wash (optional)
- Pecan halves for topping (optional)

Instructions:

Prepare Bulgur:
- Place the bulgur in a heatproof bowl.
- Pour the boiling water over the bulgur, cover the bowl, and let it sit for about 30 minutes or until the bulgur has absorbed the water and is tender.

Activate Yeast:
- In a small bowl, combine the warm water and honey (or maple syrup).
- Sprinkle the yeast over the water and let it sit for about 5-10 minutes until it becomes frothy.

Mix Dough:
- In a large mixing bowl, combine the bread flour and salt.
- Add the soaked bulgur, chopped pecans, activated yeast mixture, and olive oil.
- Mix until a dough forms.

Knead Dough:
- Turn the dough out onto a floured surface and knead for about 8-10 minutes until it becomes smooth and elastic.

First Rise:
- Place the dough in a greased bowl, cover it with a clean kitchen towel, and let it rise in a warm place for about 1-1.5 hours or until it doubles in size.

Shape and Second Rise:
- Punch down the risen dough and shape it into a loaf.
- Place the shaped dough in a greased and floured loaf pan.

- Cover and let it rise again for about 45-60 minutes.

Preheat Oven:
- Preheat your oven to 375°F (190°C).

Egg Wash and Topping (Optional):
- Beat an egg and brush it over the risen loaf for a shiny finish.
- Optionally, place pecan halves on top of the loaf.

Bake:
- Bake in the preheated oven for 30-35 minutes or until the loaf is golden brown and sounds hollow when tapped.

Cool:
- Allow the bread to cool in the pan for 10 minutes, then transfer it to a wire rack to cool completely before slicing.

Enjoy your flavorful Bulgur and Pecan Loaf! This bread is great for sandwiches or as a tasty accompaniment to soups and salads.

Kamut and Sesame Seed Bread

Ingredients:

- 2 cups Kamut flour
- 1 cup bread flour
- 1/2 cup sesame seeds, plus extra for topping
- 1 packet (2 1/4 teaspoons) active dry yeast
- 1 1/2 teaspoons salt
- 1 tablespoon honey or maple syrup
- 1 1/4 cups warm water (around 110°F or 43°C)
- 2 tablespoons olive oil

Instructions:

Activate Yeast:
- In a small bowl, combine the warm water and honey (or maple syrup).
- Sprinkle the yeast over the water and let it sit for about 5-10 minutes until it becomes frothy.

Mix Dough:
- In a large mixing bowl, combine the Kamut flour, bread flour, sesame seeds, and salt.
- Add the activated yeast mixture and olive oil.
- Mix until a dough forms.

Knead Dough:
- Turn the dough out onto a floured surface and knead for about 8-10 minutes until it becomes smooth and elastic.

First Rise:
- Place the dough in a greased bowl, cover it with a clean kitchen towel, and let it rise in a warm place for about 1-1.5 hours or until it doubles in size.

Shape and Second Rise:
- Punch down the risen dough and shape it into a loaf.
- Place the shaped dough in a greased and floured loaf pan.
- Cover and let it rise again for about 45-60 minutes.

Preheat Oven:
- Preheat your oven to 375°F (190°C).

Top with Sesame Seeds:
- Optionally, brush the top of the risen loaf with water and sprinkle additional sesame seeds for a decorative touch.

Bake:

- Bake in the preheated oven for 30-35 minutes or until the loaf is golden brown and sounds hollow when tapped.

Cool:
- Allow the bread to cool in the pan for 10 minutes, then transfer it to a wire rack to cool completely before slicing.

Enjoy your homemade Kamut and Sesame Seed Bread! It's perfect for sandwiches or served alongside soups and salads.

Einkorn and Poppy Seed Bread

Ingredients:

- 2 cups einkorn flour
- 1 cup bread flour
- 1/4 cup poppy seeds
- 1 packet (2 1/4 teaspoons) active dry yeast
- 1 1/2 teaspoons salt
- 1 tablespoon honey or maple syrup
- 1 1/4 cups warm water (around 110°F or 43°C)
- 2 tablespoons olive oil

Instructions:

Activate Yeast:
- In a small bowl, combine the warm water and honey (or maple syrup).
- Sprinkle the yeast over the water and let it sit for about 5-10 minutes until it becomes frothy.

Mix Dough:
- In a large mixing bowl, combine the einkorn flour, bread flour, poppy seeds, and salt.
- Add the activated yeast mixture and olive oil.
- Mix until a dough forms.

Knead Dough:
- Turn the dough out onto a floured surface and knead for about 8-10 minutes until it becomes smooth and elastic.

First Rise:
- Place the dough in a greased bowl, cover it with a clean kitchen towel, and let it rise in a warm place for about 1-1.5 hours or until it doubles in size.

Shape and Second Rise:
- Punch down the risen dough and shape it into a loaf.
- Place the shaped dough in a greased and floured loaf pan.
- Cover and let it rise again for about 45-60 minutes.

Preheat Oven:
- Preheat your oven to 375°F (190°C).

Bake:
- Bake in the preheated oven for 30-35 minutes or until the loaf is golden brown and sounds hollow when tapped.

Cool:

- Allow the bread to cool in the pan for 10 minutes, then transfer it to a wire rack to cool completely before slicing.

Enjoy your homemade Einkorn and Poppy Seed Bread! It has a unique flavor and texture that makes it a great choice for both sweet and savory toppings.

Farro and Hazelnut Bread

Ingredients:

- 2 cups farro flour
- 1 cup bread flour
- 1/2 cup chopped hazelnuts
- 1 packet (2 1/4 teaspoons) active dry yeast
- 1 1/2 teaspoons salt
- 1 tablespoon honey or maple syrup
- 1 1/4 cups warm water (around 110°F or 43°C)
- 2 tablespoons olive oil

Instructions:

Activate Yeast:
- In a small bowl, combine the warm water and honey (or maple syrup).
- Sprinkle the yeast over the water and let it sit for about 5-10 minutes until it becomes frothy.

Mix Dough:
- In a large mixing bowl, combine the farro flour, bread flour, chopped hazelnuts, and salt.
- Add the activated yeast mixture and olive oil.
- Mix until a dough forms.

Knead Dough:
- Turn the dough out onto a floured surface and knead for about 8-10 minutes until it becomes smooth and elastic.

First Rise:
- Place the dough in a greased bowl, cover it with a clean kitchen towel, and let it rise in a warm place for about 1-1.5 hours or until it doubles in size.

Shape and Second Rise:
- Punch down the risen dough and shape it into a loaf.
- Place the shaped dough in a greased and floured loaf pan.
- Cover and let it rise again for about 45-60 minutes.

Preheat Oven:
- Preheat your oven to 375°F (190°C).

Bake:
- Bake in the preheated oven for 30-35 minutes or until the loaf is golden brown and sounds hollow when tapped.

Cool:

- Allow the bread to cool in the pan for 10 minutes, then transfer it to a wire rack to cool completely before slicing.

Enjoy your homemade Farro and Hazelnut Bread! The combination of farro and hazelnuts adds a rich, earthy flavor to the bread, making it a perfect choice for sandwiches or as a side for soups and salads.

Millet and Cranberry Bread

Ingredients:

- 2 cups millet flour
- 1 cup bread flour
- 1/2 cup dried cranberries
- 1 packet (2 1/4 teaspoons) active dry yeast
- 1 1/2 teaspoons salt
- 1 tablespoon honey or maple syrup
- 1 1/4 cups warm water (around 110°F or 43°C)
- 2 tablespoons olive oil

Instructions:

Activate Yeast:
- In a small bowl, combine the warm water and honey (or maple syrup).
- Sprinkle the yeast over the water and let it sit for about 5-10 minutes until it becomes frothy.

Mix Dough:
- In a large mixing bowl, combine the millet flour, bread flour, dried cranberries, and salt.
- Add the activated yeast mixture and olive oil.
- Mix until a dough forms.

Knead Dough:
- Turn the dough out onto a floured surface and knead for about 8-10 minutes until it becomes smooth and elastic.

First Rise:
- Place the dough in a greased bowl, cover it with a clean kitchen towel, and let it rise in a warm place for about 1-1.5 hours or until it doubles in size.

Shape and Second Rise:
- Punch down the risen dough and shape it into a loaf.
- Place the shaped dough in a greased and floured loaf pan.
- Cover and let it rise again for about 45-60 minutes.

Preheat Oven:
- Preheat your oven to 375°F (190°C).

Bake:
- Bake in the preheated oven for 30-35 minutes or until the loaf is golden brown and sounds hollow when tapped.

Cool:

- Allow the bread to cool in the pan for 10 minutes, then transfer it to a wire rack to cool completely before slicing.

Enjoy your homemade Millet and Cranberry Bread! The millet adds a nutty crunch, while the cranberries provide a burst of sweetness, creating a unique and delicious bread perfect for breakfast or as a snack.

Emmer and Almond Loaf

Ingredients:

- 2 cups emmer flour
- 1 cup bread flour
- 1/2 cup chopped almonds
- 1 packet (2 1/4 teaspoons) active dry yeast
- 1 1/2 teaspoons salt
- 1 tablespoon honey or maple syrup
- 1 1/4 cups warm water (around 110°F or 43°C)
- 2 tablespoons olive oil

Instructions:

Activate Yeast:
- In a small bowl, combine the warm water and honey (or maple syrup).
- Sprinkle the yeast over the water and let it sit for about 5-10 minutes until it becomes frothy.

Mix Dough:
- In a large mixing bowl, combine the emmer flour, bread flour, chopped almonds, and salt.
- Add the activated yeast mixture and olive oil.
- Mix until a dough forms.

Knead Dough:
- Turn the dough out onto a floured surface and knead for about 8-10 minutes until it becomes smooth and elastic.

First Rise:
- Place the dough in a greased bowl, cover it with a clean kitchen towel, and let it rise in a warm place for about 1-1.5 hours or until it doubles in size.

Shape and Second Rise:
- Punch down the risen dough and shape it into a loaf.
- Place the shaped dough in a greased and floured loaf pan.
- Cover and let it rise again for about 45-60 minutes.

Preheat Oven:
- Preheat your oven to 375°F (190°C).

Bake:
- Bake in the preheated oven for 30-35 minutes or until the loaf is golden brown and sounds hollow when tapped.

Cool:

- Allow the bread to cool in the pan for 10 minutes, then transfer it to a wire rack to cool completely before slicing.

Enjoy your homemade Emmer and Almond Loaf! This bread is perfect for sandwiches or enjoyed with a smear of almond butter for a delicious and nutritious treat.

Sorghum and Pine Nut Bread

Ingredients:

- 2 cups sorghum flour
- 1 cup bread flour
- 1/2 cup pine nuts
- 1 packet (2 1/4 teaspoons) active dry yeast
- 1 1/2 teaspoons salt
- 1 tablespoon honey or maple syrup
- 1 1/4 cups warm water (around 110°F or 43°C)
- 2 tablespoons olive oil

Instructions:

Activate Yeast:
- In a small bowl, combine the warm water and honey (or maple syrup).
- Sprinkle the yeast over the water and let it sit for about 5-10 minutes until it becomes frothy.

Mix Dough:
- In a large mixing bowl, combine the sorghum flour, bread flour, pine nuts, and salt.
- Add the activated yeast mixture and olive oil.
- Mix until a dough forms.

Knead Dough:
- Turn the dough out onto a floured surface and knead for about 8-10 minutes until it becomes smooth and elastic.

First Rise:
- Place the dough in a greased bowl, cover it with a clean kitchen towel, and let it rise in a warm place for about 1-1.5 hours or until it doubles in size.

Shape and Second Rise:
- Punch down the risen dough and shape it into a loaf.
- Place the shaped dough in a greased and floured loaf pan.
- Cover and let it rise again for about 45-60 minutes.

Preheat Oven:
- Preheat your oven to 375°F (190°C).

Bake:
- Bake in the preheated oven for 30-35 minutes or until the loaf is golden brown and sounds hollow when tapped.

Cool:

- Allow the bread to cool in the pan for 10 minutes, then transfer it to a wire rack to cool completely before slicing.

Enjoy your homemade Sorghum and Pine Nut Bread! This bread has a unique flavor profile, making it a wonderful addition to your bread repertoire. Consider pairing it with cheeses or using it for open-faced sandwiches with savory or sweet toppings.

Whole Spelt Bagels

Ingredients:

- 3 1/2 cups whole spelt flour
- 1 tablespoon honey or maple syrup
- 1 1/2 teaspoons salt
- 1 packet (2 1/4 teaspoons) active dry yeast
- 1 1/4 cups warm water (around 110°F or 43°C)
- 1 tablespoon olive oil (optional, for a softer crust)
- Toppings: sesame seeds, poppy seeds, or coarse salt (optional)

Instructions:

Activate Yeast:
- In a small bowl, combine the warm water and honey (or maple syrup).
- Sprinkle the yeast over the water and let it sit for about 5-10 minutes until it becomes frothy.

Mix Dough:
- In a large mixing bowl, combine the whole spelt flour and salt.
- Add the activated yeast mixture and mix until a dough forms.

Knead Dough:
- Turn the dough out onto a floured surface and knead for about 8-10 minutes until it becomes smooth and elastic.

First Rise:
- Place the dough in a greased bowl, cover it with a clean kitchen towel, and let it rise in a warm place for about 1-1.5 hours or until it doubles in size.

Divide and Shape:
- Preheat your oven to 425°F (220°C).
- Punch down the risen dough and divide it into 8 equal portions.
- Shape each portion into a ball and then poke a hole through the center to form a bagel shape.

Second Rise:
- Place the shaped bagels on a parchment-lined baking sheet.
- Cover and let them rise for another 15-20 minutes.

Boil Bagels:
- In a large pot, bring water to a boil.
- Carefully drop the bagels into the boiling water, boiling each side for about 1-2 minutes.

Optional: Add Toppings:

- If desired, sprinkle sesame seeds, poppy seeds, or coarse salt on the bagels while they are still wet.

Bake:
- Transfer the boiled bagels back to the baking sheet.
- Bake in the preheated oven for 15-20 minutes or until golden brown.

Cool:
- Allow the bagels to cool on a wire rack before slicing.

Enjoy your whole spelt bagels! They're a wholesome and delicious option for breakfast or as a base for your favorite toppings.

Sunflower Seed Rye Rolls

Ingredients:

- 2 cups dark rye flour
- 1 cup bread flour
- 1/2 cup sunflower seeds (plus extra for topping)
- 1 packet (2 1/4 teaspoons) active dry yeast
- 1 1/2 teaspoons salt
- 1 tablespoon honey or molasses
- 1 1/4 cups warm water (around 110°F or 43°C)
- 2 tablespoons olive oil

Instructions:

Activate Yeast:
- In a small bowl, combine the warm water and honey (or molasses).
- Sprinkle the yeast over the water and let it sit for about 5-10 minutes until it becomes frothy.

Mix Dough:
- In a large mixing bowl, combine the rye flour, bread flour, sunflower seeds, and salt.
- Add the activated yeast mixture and olive oil.
- Mix until a dough forms.

Knead Dough:
- Turn the dough out onto a floured surface and knead for about 8-10 minutes until it becomes smooth and elastic.

First Rise:
- Place the dough in a greased bowl, cover it with a clean kitchen towel, and let it rise in a warm place for about 1-1.5 hours or until it doubles in size.

Shape Rolls:
- Punch down the risen dough and divide it into 8 equal portions.
- Shape each portion into a round roll.

Second Rise:
- Place the shaped rolls on a parchment-lined baking sheet.
- Cover and let them rise for another 30-45 minutes.

Preheat Oven:
- Preheat your oven to 375°F (190°C).

Top with Sunflower Seeds:

- Optionally, brush the tops of the rolls with water and sprinkle additional sunflower seeds for a decorative touch.

Bake:
- Bake in the preheated oven for 20-25 minutes or until the rolls are golden brown and sound hollow when tapped.

Cool:
- Allow the rolls to cool on a wire rack before serving.

Enjoy your homemade Sunflower Seed Rye Rolls! They make a delicious and nutritious addition to your meals, and you can use them for sandwiches or as a side with soups and salads.

Whole Wheat Sourdough Boule

Ingredients:

For the Sourdough Starter:

- 1/2 cup active sourdough starter
- 1 cup whole wheat flour
- 1/2 cup water (filtered or dechlorinated)

For the Dough:

- 2 1/2 cups whole wheat flour
- 1 1/2 teaspoons salt
- 1 cup water (filtered or dechlorinated)

Instructions:

Day 1: Prepare the Sourdough Starter

Create the Starter:
- In a bowl, mix the active sourdough starter, whole wheat flour, and water.
- Ensure it has a thick, paste-like consistency.
- Cover loosely and let it sit at room temperature for about 12 hours or overnight.

Day 2: Mix the Dough

Combine Ingredients:
- In a large mixing bowl, combine the fed sourdough starter, whole wheat flour, salt, and water.
- Mix until a shaggy dough forms.

Autolyse:
- Cover the bowl and let it rest for 30 minutes to 1 hour. This allows the flour to absorb the water and the gluten to start developing.

Day 2 (Continued): Bulk Fermentation and Shaping

Bulk Fermentation:
- Perform a series of stretch-and-folds every 30 minutes for the first 2 hours. Wet your hands to prevent sticking.
- Allow the dough to ferment at room temperature for a total of 4-6 hours, or until it has increased in volume and has a bubbly texture.

Shape the Dough:

- Flour your hands and the work surface.
- Gently shape the dough into a boule (round shape).
- Place the shaped dough seam side down in a well-floured proofing basket or a bowl lined with a floured kitchen towel.

Final Rise (Proofing):
- Cover the dough with a cloth and let it rise for 2-4 hours or until it has visibly expanded and is puffy.

Day 2 (Continued): Baking

Preheat the Oven:
- Preheat your oven to 450°F (232°C) with a Dutch oven inside.

Transfer and Score the Dough:
- Carefully transfer the risen dough to the preheated Dutch oven.
- Score the top of the dough with a sharp knife or lame.

Bake with Lid On:
- Cover the Dutch oven with its lid and bake for 20-25 minutes.

Bake with Lid Off:
- Remove the lid and continue baking for an additional 20-25 minutes or until the bread is deep golden brown and sounds hollow when tapped on the bottom.

Cool:
- Allow the bread to cool on a wire rack before slicing.

Enjoy your homemade whole wheat sourdough boule! Feel free to adjust the hydration, fermentation times, or other factors based on your preferences and the characteristics of your sourdough starter.

Flax and Chia Swirl Bread

Ingredients:

For the Dough:

- 3 1/2 cups all-purpose flour
- 1 packet (2 1/4 teaspoons) active dry yeast
- 1 1/4 cups warm milk (around 110°F or 43°C)
- 2 tablespoons honey or maple syrup
- 2 tablespoons melted butter or oil
- 1 teaspoon salt

For the Flax and Chia Swirl:

- 1/2 cup ground flaxseeds
- 1/4 cup chia seeds
- 1/4 cup water
- 2 tablespoons honey or maple syrup

Instructions:

For the Dough:

Activate Yeast:
- In a bowl, combine warm milk and honey (or maple syrup). Sprinkle the yeast over the mixture and let it sit for 5-10 minutes until frothy.

Combine Ingredients:
- In a large mixing bowl, combine the activated yeast mixture, flour, melted butter (or oil), and salt.
- Mix until a dough forms.

Knead Dough:
- Turn the dough out onto a floured surface and knead for about 8-10 minutes until it becomes smooth and elastic.

First Rise:
- Place the dough in a greased bowl, cover it with a clean kitchen towel, and let it rise in a warm place for about 1-1.5 hours or until it doubles in size.

For the Flax and Chia Swirl:

Prepare Flax and Chia Mixture:

- In a small bowl, mix ground flaxseeds, chia seeds, water, and honey (or maple syrup) to form a thick paste.

Assemble and Second Rise:

Roll Out Dough:
- Punch down the risen dough and roll it out into a rectangle on a floured surface.

Spread Flax and Chia Mixture:
- Evenly spread the flax and chia mixture over the rolled-out dough.

Roll into a Log:
- Starting from one of the longer edges, tightly roll the dough into a log.

Place in Loaf Pan:
- Place the rolled dough into a greased and floured loaf pan, seam side down.

Second Rise:
- Cover the pan with a kitchen towel and let it rise for an additional 45-60 minutes.

Bake:

Preheat Oven:
- Preheat your oven to 350°F (175°C).

Bake:
- Bake the bread in the preheated oven for 30-35 minutes or until it's golden brown and sounds hollow when tapped on the bottom.

Cool:
- Allow the bread to cool in the pan for 10 minutes, then transfer it to a wire rack to cool completely before slicing.

Enjoy your Flax and Chia Swirl Bread! This nutritious and flavorful bread is perfect for sandwiches or toast, and the swirl adds a unique touch to each slice.

Three-Seed Whole Grain Flatbread

Ingredients:

- 1 cup whole wheat flour
- 1/2 cup all-purpose flour
- 1/2 cup oat flour
- 1 teaspoon baking powder
- 1/2 teaspoon salt
- 1 tablespoon chia seeds
- 1 tablespoon flaxseeds
- 1 tablespoon sunflower seeds
- 1 cup warm water
- 2 tablespoons olive oil

Instructions:

In a large mixing bowl, combine the whole wheat flour, all-purpose flour, oat flour, baking powder, and salt.
Add chia seeds, flaxseeds, and sunflower seeds to the flour mixture. Mix well to distribute the seeds evenly.
Make a well in the center of the dry ingredients and pour in the warm water and olive oil.
Gradually incorporate the wet ingredients into the dry ingredients, mixing until a dough forms. If the dough is too sticky, you can add a bit more flour.
Knead the dough on a floured surface for a few minutes until it becomes smooth and elastic.
Divide the dough into small balls, about golf ball-sized.
Roll out each ball into a flatbread, about 1/8 inch thick. You can use a rolling pin for this.
Heat a skillet or griddle over medium heat. Once hot, place a flatbread on the skillet and cook for 1-2 minutes on each side, or until golden brown and cooked through.
Repeat the process with the remaining dough balls.
Serve the three-seed whole grain flatbread warm, with your favorite toppings or as a side to your favorite dishes.

Feel free to customize this recipe by adding herbs, spices, or other seeds according to your preferences. Enjoy your nutritious and delicious flatbread!

Oat Bran and Date Loaf

Ingredients:

- 1 cup oat bran
- 1 cup boiling water
- 1 cup chopped dates
- 1/4 cup unsalted butter, softened
- 1/2 cup brown sugar (or a sweetener of your choice)
- 1 large egg
- 1 teaspoon vanilla extract
- 1 cup all-purpose flour
- 1 teaspoon baking soda
- 1/2 teaspoon baking powder
- 1/2 teaspoon salt
- 1/2 cup chopped nuts (such as walnuts or pecans), optional

Instructions:

Preheat your oven to 350°F (175°C). Grease and flour a loaf pan.
In a bowl, combine the oat bran and boiling water. Let it sit for about 5-10 minutes to allow the oat bran to absorb the water.
In a separate bowl, cream together the softened butter and brown sugar until light and fluffy.
Add the egg and vanilla extract to the butter and sugar mixture. Mix well.
In another bowl, whisk together the all-purpose flour, baking soda, baking powder, and salt.
Gradually add the dry ingredients to the wet ingredients, mixing just until combined.
Fold in the soaked oat bran and chopped dates. If you're using nuts, add them to the batter as well.
Pour the batter into the prepared loaf pan and smooth the top.
Bake in the preheated oven for 40-50 minutes or until a toothpick inserted into the center comes out clean.

Allow the oat bran and date loaf to cool in the pan for about 10 minutes, then transfer it to a wire rack to cool completely.
Once cooled, slice and enjoy!

This loaf is wonderfully moist and makes for a delightful snack or breakfast option. Feel free to adjust the sweetness or add spices like cinnamon for extra flavor.

Ancient Grains Ciabatta

Ingredients:

- 2 cups bread flour
- 1 cup whole wheat flour
- 1/2 cup spelt flour
- 1/4 cup quinoa flour
- 1 1/2 teaspoons salt
- 1 teaspoon active dry yeast
- 1 1/2 cups lukewarm water
- 2 tablespoons olive oil
- 1/4 cup amaranth seeds (optional, for topping)
- 1/4 cup millet seeds (optional, for topping)

Instructions:

In a large mixing bowl, combine the bread flour, whole wheat flour, spelt flour, quinoa flour, and salt.

In a small bowl, dissolve the yeast in lukewarm water. Let it sit for about 5 minutes until it becomes frothy.

Add the activated yeast mixture and olive oil to the flour mixture. Stir until a rough dough forms.

Turn the dough onto a floured surface and knead for about 10-15 minutes, or until the dough becomes smooth and elastic. You may need to add extra flour if the dough is too sticky.

Place the dough in a lightly oiled bowl, cover it with a damp cloth, and let it rise in a warm place for 1-2 hours or until it has doubled in size.

Preheat your oven to 450°F (230°C). If you have a pizza stone, place it in the oven to heat.

Punch down the risen dough and turn it out onto a floured surface. Divide the dough into two equal portions.

Shape each portion into a rectangular or oval shape, trying to maintain the characteristic flat shape of ciabatta.

If desired, sprinkle the tops of the loaves with amaranth seeds and millet seeds, gently pressing them into the dough.

Carefully transfer the shaped loaves onto a parchment-lined baking sheet or a preheated pizza stone.

Bake in the preheated oven for 20-25 minutes or until the ciabatta loaves are golden brown and sound hollow when tapped on the bottom.
Allow the loaves to cool on a wire rack before slicing.

Enjoy your Ancient Grains Ciabatta with its nutty flavor and added nutritional benefits from the ancient grains!

Muesli Bread with Dried Fruit

Ingredients:

- 2 cups all-purpose flour
- 1 cup whole wheat flour
- 1/2 cup rolled oats
- 1/2 cup muesli (with nuts and seeds)
- 1/4 cup brown sugar
- 1 teaspoon salt
- 1 tablespoon active dry yeast
- 1 1/4 cups warm water (around 110°F or 43°C)
- 1/4 cup olive oil
- 1/2 cup mixed dried fruits (raisins, cranberries, apricots, etc.)
- Additional oats for topping (optional)

Instructions:

In a small bowl, dissolve the brown sugar and yeast in warm water. Let it sit for about 5 minutes until it becomes frothy.

In a large mixing bowl, combine the all-purpose flour, whole wheat flour, rolled oats, muesli, and salt.

Add the yeast mixture and olive oil to the dry ingredients. Stir until a rough dough forms.

Turn the dough onto a floured surface and knead for about 10 minutes, or until the dough becomes smooth and elastic. You may need to add extra flour if the dough is too sticky.

Place the dough in a lightly oiled bowl, cover it with a damp cloth, and let it rise in a warm place for 1-2 hours or until it has doubled in size.

Punch down the risen dough and turn it out onto a floured surface. Flatten the dough and sprinkle the dried fruits over it. Fold the dough over and knead it briefly to distribute the fruits evenly.

Shape the dough into a loaf and place it in a greased and floured loaf pan.

If desired, sprinkle additional oats on top of the loaf.

Cover the loaf with a damp cloth and let it rise for another 30-45 minutes, or until it reaches just above the edges of the pan.

Preheat your oven to 375°F (190°C).

Bake the muesli bread in the preheated oven for 30-40 minutes, or until the top is golden brown and the bread sounds hollow when tapped on the bottom.

Allow the bread to cool in the pan for a few minutes before transferring it to a wire rack to cool completely.

Slice and enjoy your Muesli Bread with Dried Fruit for a delicious and nutritious treat!

Quinoa and Amaranth Focaccia

Ingredients:

For the Dough:

- 2 1/4 teaspoons (1 packet) active dry yeast
- 1 teaspoon sugar
- 1 1/2 cups warm water (about 110°F or 43°C)
- 4 cups all-purpose flour
- 1/2 cup quinoa flour
- 1/4 cup amaranth flour
- 1 teaspoon salt
- 1/4 cup olive oil, plus extra for drizzling

For Topping:

- 2 tablespoons cooked quinoa
- 2 tablespoons cooked amaranth
- 2 tablespoons fresh rosemary, chopped
- Coarse sea salt, to taste
- Olive oil, for drizzling

Instructions:

In a small bowl, combine the active dry yeast, sugar, and warm water. Allow it to sit for about 5-10 minutes, or until it becomes frothy.

In a large mixing bowl, combine the all-purpose flour, quinoa flour, amaranth flour, and salt.

Make a well in the center of the flour mixture and pour in the yeast mixture and olive oil. Stir until a dough forms.

Turn the dough onto a floured surface and knead for about 8-10 minutes, or until it becomes smooth and elastic. Add more flour if the dough is too sticky.

Place the dough in a lightly oiled bowl, cover it with a damp cloth, and let it rise in a warm place for about 1-1.5 hours, or until it doubles in size.

Preheat your oven to 425°F (220°C). Grease a baking sheet or line it with parchment paper.

Punch down the risen dough and transfer it to the prepared baking sheet. Press the dough out to the edges of the pan.

Drizzle olive oil over the top of the dough and use your fingers to dimple the surface.

Sprinkle the cooked quinoa, cooked amaranth, and chopped rosemary evenly over the dough. Press them down gently.

Sprinkle coarse sea salt over the top according to your taste.

Bake in the preheated oven for 20-25 minutes or until the focaccia is golden brown and sounds hollow when tapped on the bottom.

Remove from the oven and drizzle with additional olive oil if desired.

Allow the focaccia to cool slightly before slicing and serving.

Enjoy your Quinoa and Amaranth Focaccia with its unique texture and flavors!

Sun-Dried Tomato and Basil Spelt Bread

Ingredients:

- 2 cups whole grain spelt flour
- 1 cup all-purpose spelt flour
- 1 1/2 teaspoons salt
- 1 tablespoon active dry yeast
- 1 tablespoon honey or maple syrup
- 1 1/4 cups warm water (about 110°F or 43°C)
- 2 tablespoons olive oil
- 1/3 cup sun-dried tomatoes, chopped
- 2 tablespoons fresh basil, finely chopped
- Additional olive oil for brushing (optional)

Instructions:

In a small bowl, combine the warm water, honey or maple syrup, and active dry yeast. Allow it to sit for about 5-10 minutes, or until it becomes frothy.

In a large mixing bowl, combine the whole grain spelt flour, all-purpose spelt flour, and salt.

Make a well in the center of the flour mixture and pour in the yeast mixture and olive oil. Stir until a dough forms.

Turn the dough onto a floured surface and knead for about 8-10 minutes, or until it becomes smooth and elastic. Add more flour if the dough is too sticky.

Place the dough in a lightly oiled bowl, cover it with a damp cloth, and let it rise in a warm place for about 1-1.5 hours, or until it doubles in size.

Preheat your oven to 375°F (190°C). Grease or line a baking sheet with parchment paper.

Punch down the risen dough and turn it out onto a floured surface.

Flatten the dough and sprinkle the chopped sun-dried tomatoes and fresh basil evenly over it. Fold the dough over and knead it briefly to distribute the tomatoes and basil.

Shape the dough into a round or oval loaf and place it on the prepared baking sheet.

Optionally, brush the top of the loaf with olive oil.

Bake in the preheated oven for 25-30 minutes, or until the bread is golden brown and sounds hollow when tapped on the bottom.

Allow the bread to cool on a wire rack before slicing.

This Sun-Dried Tomato and Basil Spelt Bread is excellent for sandwiches, toast, or as a side to soups and salads. Enjoy the unique flavors of sun-dried tomatoes and fresh basil in every bite!

Buckwheat and Almond Biscuits

Ingredients:

- 1 cup buckwheat flour
- 1/2 cup almond flour
- 1/4 cup coconut flour
- 1 teaspoon baking powder
- 1/2 teaspoon baking soda
- 1/4 teaspoon salt
- 1/4 cup unsalted butter, cold and cut into small pieces
- 1/4 cup maple syrup or honey
- 1 large egg
- 1 teaspoon vanilla extract
- 1/3 cup plain yogurt or buttermilk
- 1/3 cup chopped almonds

Instructions:

Preheat your oven to 375°F (190°C). Line a baking sheet with parchment paper.
In a large bowl, whisk together the buckwheat flour, almond flour, coconut flour, baking powder, baking soda, and salt.
Add the cold butter pieces to the dry ingredients. Use a pastry cutter or your fingers to cut the butter into the flour until the mixture resembles coarse crumbs.
In a separate bowl, whisk together the maple syrup or honey, egg, vanilla extract, and yogurt or buttermilk.
Pour the wet ingredients into the dry ingredients and stir until just combined. Fold in the chopped almonds.
Turn the dough out onto a floured surface and gently knead it a few times until it comes together.
Roll out the dough to about 1/2-inch thickness. Use a biscuit cutter to cut out biscuits and place them on the prepared baking sheet.
Gather any remaining dough, re-roll, and cut out more biscuits.
Bake in the preheated oven for 12-15 minutes or until the biscuits are golden brown.
Allow the biscuits to cool on a wire rack before serving.

These buckwheat and almond biscuits are delicious served warm with butter, honey, or your favorite jam. Enjoy the nutty and wholesome flavor!

Walnut and Fig Whole Grain Bread

Ingredients:

- 1 1/2 cups whole wheat flour
- 1 cup all-purpose flour
- 1/2 cup rolled oats
- 1 teaspoon baking soda
- 1/2 teaspoon baking powder
- 1/2 teaspoon salt
- 1/2 cup unsalted butter, softened
- 1/2 cup brown sugar or coconut sugar
- 2 large eggs
- 1 teaspoon vanilla extract
- 1 cup buttermilk
- 1 cup chopped dried figs
- 1 cup chopped walnuts

Instructions:

Preheat your oven to 350°F (175°C). Grease and flour a standard-sized loaf pan.
In a bowl, whisk together the whole wheat flour, all-purpose flour, rolled oats, baking soda, baking powder, and salt.
In another large bowl, cream together the softened butter and sugar until light and fluffy.
Add the eggs one at a time, beating well after each addition. Stir in the vanilla extract.
Gradually add the dry ingredients to the wet ingredients, alternating with the buttermilk. Begin and end with the dry ingredients, mixing until just combined.
Fold in the chopped dried figs and walnuts, reserving a small amount of each for topping.
Pour the batter into the prepared loaf pan, spreading it evenly. Sprinkle the reserved figs and walnuts on top.
Bake in the preheated oven for 50-60 minutes or until a toothpick inserted into the center comes out clean.
Allow the bread to cool in the pan for about 10 minutes before transferring it to a wire rack to cool completely.
Once cooled, slice and enjoy your Walnut and Fig Whole Grain Bread!

This bread is perfect for breakfast or as a snack, and the combination of walnuts and figs adds a delicious texture and flavor. Feel free to customize the recipe according to your preferences!

Pumpkin Seed Rye Sourdough

Ingredients:

Leaven:

- 1/4 cup active sourdough starter
- 1/2 cup whole wheat flour
- 1/2 cup water

Dough:

- 1 cup rye flour
- 2 cups bread flour
- 1 1/4 cups water
- 1 1/2 teaspoons salt
- 1/2 cup pumpkin seeds (plus extra for topping)

Instructions:

Leaven (prepare the night before baking):

In a jar, mix the sourdough starter, whole wheat flour, and water. Cover loosely and let it sit at room temperature for 8-12 hours or overnight until bubbly and active.

Dough:

In a large bowl, combine the leaven, rye flour, bread flour, water, and salt. Mix until just combined.
Add pumpkin seeds to the dough and mix until they are evenly distributed.
Knead the dough on a floured surface for about 10 minutes until it becomes smooth and elastic.
Place the dough back into the bowl, cover with a damp cloth, and let it rest for about 30 minutes.

Perform a series of stretch and folds every 30 minutes for the first 2 hours of bulk fermentation. To do a stretch and fold, grab one side of the dough, stretch it up, and fold it over the center. Repeat with the other three sides.

After bulk fermentation (2-3 hours, or until the dough has visibly risen), shape the dough into a round or oval shape.

Place the shaped dough into a well-floured proofing basket, seam side down. Cover the basket with a cloth or plastic wrap and let it proof in the refrigerator overnight (about 8-12 hours).

Preheat your oven to 450°F (230°C) and place a Dutch oven or baking stone inside to heat.

Remove the dough from the refrigerator and let it come to room temperature while the oven heats.

Score the top of the dough with a sharp knife or razor blade. Sprinkle additional pumpkin seeds on top.

Carefully transfer the dough into the preheated Dutch oven or onto the baking stone. Cover with the lid or use a large pot to cover.

Bake covered for 20 minutes, then uncover and bake for an additional 20-25 minutes or until the crust is golden brown and the bread sounds hollow when tapped on the bottom.

Allow the Pumpkin Seed Rye Sourdough to cool on a wire rack before slicing.

Enjoy your homemade Pumpkin Seed Rye Sourdough with its rich flavor and crunchy pumpkin seed crust!

Millet and Blueberry Breakfast Bread

Ingredients:

- 1 cup all-purpose flour
- 1 cup whole wheat flour
- 1/2 cup millet flour
- 1 teaspoon baking powder
- 1/2 teaspoon baking soda
- 1/2 teaspoon salt
- 1/2 cup unsalted butter, softened
- 1/2 cup granulated sugar
- 2 large eggs
- 1 teaspoon vanilla extract
- 1 cup plain Greek yogurt
- 1 cup fresh or frozen blueberries (if using frozen, do not thaw)
- 1/2 cup cooked millet (cooled)
- Zest of 1 lemon (optional)

Instructions:

Preheat your oven to 350°F (175°C). Grease and flour a standard-sized loaf pan.
In a bowl, whisk together the all-purpose flour, whole wheat flour, millet flour, baking powder, baking soda, and salt.
In another large bowl, cream together the softened butter and sugar until light and fluffy.
Add the eggs one at a time, beating well after each addition. Stir in the vanilla extract.
Gradually add the dry ingredients to the wet ingredients, alternating with the Greek yogurt. Begin and end with the dry ingredients, mixing until just combined.
Gently fold in the cooked millet and blueberries until evenly distributed throughout the batter. If using, add the lemon zest.
Pour the batter into the prepared loaf pan, spreading it evenly.
Bake in the preheated oven for 50-60 minutes or until a toothpick inserted into the center comes out clean.
Allow the bread to cool in the pan for about 10 minutes before transferring it to a wire rack to cool completely.
Once cooled, slice and enjoy your Millet and Blueberry Breakfast Bread!

This bread is great on its own, or you can serve it with a dollop of Greek yogurt and a drizzle of honey for a delightful breakfast treat. The millet adds a wonderful crunch, and the blueberries provide bursts of sweetness.

Whole Wheat Pita Bread

Ingredients:

- 2 1/4 teaspoons (1 packet) active dry yeast
- 1 teaspoon sugar
- 1 1/4 cups warm water (about 110°F or 43°C)
- 2 cups whole wheat flour
- 1 cup all-purpose flour
- 1 teaspoon salt
- 1 tablespoon olive oil

Instructions:

In a small bowl, combine the active dry yeast, sugar, and warm water. Allow it to sit for about 5-10 minutes until it becomes frothy.

In a large mixing bowl, combine the whole wheat flour, all-purpose flour, and salt. Make a well in the center of the flour mixture and pour in the yeast mixture and olive oil. Stir until a dough forms.

Turn the dough onto a floured surface and knead for about 5-8 minutes, or until it becomes smooth and elastic. Add more flour if the dough is too sticky.

Place the dough in a lightly oiled bowl, cover it with a damp cloth, and let it rise in a warm place for about 1-2 hours, or until it has doubled in size.

Preheat your oven to 475°F (245°C). If you have a pizza stone, place it in the oven to heat.

Punch down the risen dough and turn it out onto a floured surface.

Divide the dough into 8 equal portions and shape each into a ball.

Roll out each ball into a circle, about 1/8 inch thick.

If using a pizza stone, carefully transfer the rolled-out dough circles onto the hot stone in the oven. If not using a stone, place the circles on a baking sheet.

Bake for 5-7 minutes, or until the pitas puff up and turn golden brown.

Remove from the oven and let them cool on a wire rack.

Your homemade whole wheat pita bread is ready to be served! Enjoy them with your favorite fillings or use them as a base for Mediterranean-style dishes.

Barley and Olive Loaf

Ingredients:

- 1 cup barley flour
- 2 cups bread flour
- 1 cup warm water (about 110°F or 43°C)
- 1 tablespoon active dry yeast
- 1 teaspoon sugar
- 1 teaspoon salt
- 2 tablespoons olive oil
- 1/2 cup pitted and chopped green or black olives (or a mix of both)
- 1 tablespoon chopped fresh rosemary (optional)

Instructions:

In a small bowl, combine the warm water, sugar, and active dry yeast. Allow it to sit for about 5-10 minutes until it becomes frothy.
In a large mixing bowl, combine the barley flour, bread flour, and salt.
Make a well in the center of the flour mixture and pour in the yeast mixture and olive oil. Stir until a dough forms.
Turn the dough onto a floured surface and knead for about 8-10 minutes, or until it becomes smooth and elastic. Add more flour if the dough is too sticky.
Place the dough in a lightly oiled bowl, cover it with a damp cloth, and let it rise in a warm place for about 1-2 hours, or until it has doubled in size.
Preheat your oven to 375°F (190°C). Grease or line a baking sheet with parchment paper.
Punch down the risen dough and turn it out onto a floured surface.
Flatten the dough and sprinkle the chopped olives (and rosemary if using) evenly over it. Fold the dough over and knead it briefly to distribute the olives.
Shape the dough into a round or oval loaf and place it on the prepared baking sheet.
Optionally, brush the top of the loaf with a bit of olive oil.
Bake in the preheated oven for 25-30 minutes, or until the bread is golden brown and sounds hollow when tapped on the bottom.
Allow the Barley and Olive Loaf to cool on a wire rack before slicing.

This bread is perfect for serving alongside soups, salads, or as a flavorful base for sandwiches. Enjoy the combination of hearty barley and savory olives in every bite!

7-Grain Dinner Rolls

Ingredients:

- 1 cup warm milk (about 110°F or 43°C)
- 2 tablespoons honey or maple syrup
- 2 1/4 teaspoons (1 packet) active dry yeast
- 2 1/2 cups 7-grain flour blend
- 1 cup all-purpose flour
- 1/4 cup unsalted butter, melted
- 1 teaspoon salt
- 1 large egg
- 1/2 cup mixed seeds (such as sunflower seeds, flaxseeds, sesame seeds, etc.), optional, for topping
- Additional melted butter for brushing (optional)

Instructions:

In a bowl, combine the warm milk and honey (or maple syrup). Sprinkle the yeast over the mixture and let it sit for about 5-10 minutes, or until it becomes frothy.
In a large mixing bowl, combine the 7-grain flour blend, all-purpose flour, melted butter, salt, and the activated yeast mixture.
Add the egg to the mixture and stir until a soft dough forms.
Turn the dough onto a floured surface and knead for about 8-10 minutes, or until it becomes smooth and elastic. Add more flour if the dough is too sticky.
Place the dough in a lightly oiled bowl, cover it with a damp cloth, and let it rise in a warm place for about 1-1.5 hours, or until it has doubled in size.
Preheat your oven to 375°F (190°C). Grease or line a baking pan.
Punch down the risen dough and turn it out onto a floured surface.
Divide the dough into equal portions and shape each into a ball. Place the rolls in the prepared baking pan, leaving a little space between them.
Optionally, brush the tops of the rolls with melted butter and sprinkle the mixed seeds over them.
Bake in the preheated oven for 15-20 minutes or until the rolls are golden brown and sound hollow when tapped on the bottom.
Allow the 7-Grain Dinner Rolls to cool on a wire rack before serving.

These dinner rolls are perfect for accompanying meals, sandwiches, or just as a snack. The combination of grains adds a rich texture and flavor to these wholesome rolls. Enjoy!

Hazelnut and Date Spelt Bread

Ingredients:

- 1 cup spelt flour
- 2 cups whole grain spelt flour
- 1 teaspoon baking powder
- 1/2 teaspoon baking soda
- 1/2 teaspoon salt
- 1 cup chopped dates
- 1 cup chopped hazelnuts
- 1 cup buttermilk
- 1/4 cup honey or maple syrup
- 2 tablespoons olive oil
- 2 large eggs
- 1 teaspoon vanilla extract

Instructions:

Preheat your oven to 350°F (175°C). Grease and flour a standard-sized loaf pan.
In a large mixing bowl, whisk together the spelt flour, whole grain spelt flour, baking powder, baking soda, and salt.
Add the chopped dates and hazelnuts to the flour mixture. Toss them to coat and ensure they are evenly distributed.
In another bowl, whisk together the buttermilk, honey (or maple syrup), olive oil, eggs, and vanilla extract.
Pour the wet ingredients into the dry ingredients. Stir until just combined; do not overmix.
Pour the batter into the prepared loaf pan, spreading it evenly.
Bake in the preheated oven for 45-55 minutes or until a toothpick inserted into the center comes out clean.
Allow the bread to cool in the pan for about 10 minutes before transferring it to a wire rack to cool completely.
Once cooled, slice and enjoy your Hazelnut and Date Spelt Bread!

This bread is rich in flavor and has a satisfying texture from the spelt flour, and the combination of hazelnuts and dates adds a wonderful sweetness and crunch. It's perfect for breakfast or as a snack.

Sweet Potato and Quinoa Bread

Ingredients:

- 1 cup cooked and mashed sweet potato
- 1 cup cooked quinoa, cooled
- 1/2 cup unsweetened applesauce
- 1/4 cup olive oil or melted coconut oil
- 1/2 cup honey or maple syrup
- 2 large eggs
- 1 teaspoon vanilla extract
- 1 1/2 cups whole wheat flour
- 1 teaspoon baking powder
- 1/2 teaspoon baking soda
- 1/2 teaspoon salt
- 1 teaspoon ground cinnamon
- 1/2 teaspoon ground nutmeg
- 1/2 cup chopped nuts or seeds (walnuts, pecans, or sunflower seeds), optional

Instructions:

Preheat your oven to 350°F (175°C). Grease and flour a standard-sized loaf pan.
In a large mixing bowl, combine the mashed sweet potato, cooked quinoa, applesauce, olive oil (or coconut oil), honey (or maple syrup), eggs, and vanilla extract. Mix well.
In a separate bowl, whisk together the whole wheat flour, baking powder, baking soda, salt, ground cinnamon, and ground nutmeg.
Gradually add the dry ingredients to the wet ingredients, stirring until just combined.
If using, fold in the chopped nuts or seeds.
Pour the batter into the prepared loaf pan, spreading it evenly.
Bake in the preheated oven for 50-60 minutes or until a toothpick inserted into the center comes out clean.
Allow the bread to cool in the pan for about 10 minutes before transferring it to a wire rack to cool completely.
Once cooled, slice and enjoy your Sweet Potato and Quinoa Bread!

This bread is moist, flavorful, and packed with wholesome ingredients. It's perfect for breakfast or as a snack. Feel free to customize it by adding raisins, dried fruits, or your favorite nuts and seeds.

Einkorn and Raisin Baguettes

Ingredients:

- 2 cups einkorn flour
- 1 cup all-purpose flour (plus extra for dusting)
- 1 1/4 cups warm water (about 110°F or 43°C)
- 1 tablespoon honey or maple syrup
- 1 1/2 teaspoons active dry yeast
- 1 teaspoon salt
- 1/2 cup raisins
- Olive oil (for greasing)
- Cornmeal (for dusting)

Instructions:

In a small bowl, combine the warm water, honey (or maple syrup), and active dry yeast. Allow it to sit for about 5-10 minutes, or until it becomes frothy.
In a large mixing bowl, combine the einkorn flour, all-purpose flour, and salt.
Make a well in the center of the flour mixture and pour in the yeast mixture. Stir until a dough forms.
Turn the dough onto a floured surface and knead for about 8-10 minutes, or until it becomes smooth and elastic. Add more flour if the dough is too sticky.
Place the dough in a lightly oiled bowl, cover it with a damp cloth, and let it rise in a warm place for about 1-2 hours, or until it has doubled in size.
Preheat your oven to 450°F (230°C). If you have a pizza stone, place it in the oven to heat.
Punch down the risen dough and turn it out onto a floured surface.
Flatten the dough and sprinkle the raisins evenly over it. Fold the dough over and knead it briefly to distribute the raisins.
Divide the dough into two equal portions.
Shape each portion into a baguette by rolling the dough and tapering the ends.
Place the baguettes on a lightly floured surface.
If using a pizza stone, sprinkle it with cornmeal. Transfer the baguettes onto the stone or onto a baking sheet.
Optionally, make diagonal cuts on the top of each baguette with a sharp knife.
Bake in the preheated oven for 20-25 minutes or until the baguettes are golden brown and sound hollow when tapped on the bottom.

Allow the Einkorn and Raisin Baguettes to cool on a wire rack before slicing.

Enjoy the wholesome and rustic flavors of einkorn flour combined with the sweetness of raisins in these delightful baguettes!

Walnut and Cranberry Multigrain Bread

Ingredients:

- 1 cup whole wheat flour
- 1 cup all-purpose flour
- 1/2 cup rolled oats
- 1/4 cup cornmeal
- 1/4 cup flaxseeds
- 1/4 cup sunflower seeds
- 1/4 cup honey or maple syrup
- 1 1/2 teaspoons active dry yeast
- 1 teaspoon salt
- 1 cup warm water (about 110°F or 43°C)
- 2 tablespoons olive oil
- 1/2 cup chopped walnuts
- 1/2 cup dried cranberries

Instructions:

In a small bowl, combine the warm water, honey (or maple syrup), and active dry yeast. Allow it to sit for about 5-10 minutes, or until it becomes frothy.

In a large mixing bowl, combine the whole wheat flour, all-purpose flour, rolled oats, cornmeal, flaxseeds, sunflower seeds, and salt.

Make a well in the center of the flour mixture and pour in the yeast mixture and olive oil. Stir until a dough forms.

Turn the dough onto a floured surface and knead for about 8-10 minutes, or until it becomes smooth and elastic. Add more flour if the dough is too sticky.

Place the dough in a lightly oiled bowl, cover it with a damp cloth, and let it rise in a warm place for about 1-2 hours, or until it has doubled in size.

Preheat your oven to 375°F (190°C). Grease or line a baking sheet with parchment paper.

Punch down the risen dough and turn it out onto a floured surface.

Flatten the dough and sprinkle the chopped walnuts and dried cranberries evenly over it. Fold the dough over and knead it briefly to distribute the nuts and cranberries.

Shape the dough into a round or oval loaf and place it on the prepared baking sheet.

Bake in the preheated oven for 30-40 minutes or until the bread is golden brown and sounds hollow when tapped on the bottom.
Allow the Walnut and Cranberry Multigrain Bread to cool on a wire rack before slicing.

This bread is perfect for toast, sandwiches, or enjoyed on its own. The combination of walnuts and cranberries adds a delightful flavor and texture to the multigrain base.

Spelt and Rosemary Fougasse

Ingredients:

- 2 1/4 teaspoons (1 packet) active dry yeast
- 1 teaspoon sugar
- 1 1/4 cups warm water (about 110°F or 43°C)
- 3 cups spelt flour
- 1 teaspoon salt
- 2 tablespoons olive oil
- 2 tablespoons fresh rosemary, finely chopped
- Additional olive oil for brushing
- Coarse sea salt for sprinkling

Instructions:

In a small bowl, combine the warm water, sugar, and active dry yeast. Allow it to sit for about 5-10 minutes or until it becomes frothy.
In a large mixing bowl, combine the spelt flour and salt.
Make a well in the center of the flour mixture and pour in the yeast mixture and olive oil. Add the chopped rosemary. Stir until a dough forms.
Turn the dough onto a floured surface and knead for about 8-10 minutes, or until it becomes smooth and elastic. Add more flour if the dough is too sticky.
Place the dough in a lightly oiled bowl, cover it with a damp cloth, and let it rise in a warm place for about 1-1.5 hours or until it doubles in size.
Preheat your oven to 450°F (230°C). If you have a pizza stone, place it in the oven to heat.
Punch down the risen dough and turn it out onto a floured surface.
Divide the dough into two equal portions.
Roll out each portion into a rough oval shape, about 1/4 to 1/2 inch thick.
Using a sharp knife or scissors, make several diagonal slashes and openings in the dough to create the traditional leaf-like pattern of a fougasse.
Carefully transfer the shaped dough onto the preheated pizza stone or onto a baking sheet lined with parchment paper.
Brush the surface of each fougasse with olive oil and sprinkle with coarse sea salt.
Bake in the preheated oven for 15-20 minutes or until the fougasse is golden brown and sounds hollow when tapped on the bottom.

Allow the Spelt and Rosemary Fougasse to cool on a wire rack before serving.

This bread is great as an appetizer, served with olive oil and balsamic vinegar, or alongside soups and salads. Enjoy the rich flavors of spelt and rosemary in every bite!

Oat and Apricot Breadsticks

Ingredients:

- 1 cup rolled oats
- 1 cup all-purpose flour
- 1 teaspoon baking powder
- 1/2 teaspoon salt
- 2 tablespoons unsalted butter, melted
- 1/4 cup honey or maple syrup
- 1/2 cup dried apricots, finely chopped
- 1/3 cup warm water (about 110°F or 43°C)

Instructions:

Preheat your oven to 375°F (190°C). Line a baking sheet with parchment paper.
In a large mixing bowl, combine the rolled oats, all-purpose flour, baking powder, and salt.
Add the melted butter, honey (or maple syrup), and chopped dried apricots to the dry ingredients. Mix well.
Gradually add the warm water to the mixture, stirring until a dough forms.
Turn the dough onto a floured surface and knead for a few minutes until it becomes smooth.
Divide the dough into equal portions. Roll each portion into a thin rope-like shape.
Place the rolled ropes onto the prepared baking sheet, leaving space between each.
Bake in the preheated oven for 12-15 minutes or until the breadsticks are golden brown.
Allow the breadsticks to cool on the baking sheet for a few minutes before transferring them to a wire rack to cool completely.
Once cooled, break or cut the breadsticks into desired lengths.

These Oat and Apricot Breadsticks are perfect for dipping into hummus, cheese, or your favorite spread. They also make a delightful addition to a cheese board or as a snack on their own. Enjoy the wholesome combination of oats and apricots in these tasty breadsticks!

Kamut and Date Nut Rolls

Ingredients:

For the Dough:

- 2 cups kamut flour
- 1 cup all-purpose flour
- 1/4 cup honey or maple syrup
- 1 packet (about 2 1/4 teaspoons) active dry yeast
- 1 cup warm water (about 110°F or 43°C)
- 1/4 cup unsalted butter, melted
- 1 teaspoon salt

For the Filling:

- 1 cup chopped dates
- 1/2 cup chopped nuts (walnuts, pecans, or almonds)
- 2 tablespoons honey or maple syrup
- 1 teaspoon ground cinnamon

Instructions:

For the Dough:

In a small bowl, combine the warm water, honey (or maple syrup), and active dry yeast. Let it sit for about 5-10 minutes until it becomes frothy.
In a large mixing bowl, combine the kamut flour, all-purpose flour, melted butter, and salt.
Add the yeast mixture to the flour mixture and stir until a dough forms.
Turn the dough onto a floured surface and knead for about 8-10 minutes, or until it becomes smooth and elastic. Add more flour if needed.
Place the dough in a lightly oiled bowl, cover it with a damp cloth, and let it rise in a warm place for about 1-2 hours or until it doubles in size.

For the Filling:

In a bowl, combine the chopped dates, chopped nuts, honey (or maple syrup), and ground cinnamon. Mix well.

Assembly:

1. Preheat your oven to 375°F (190°C). Grease a baking dish.
2. Punch down the risen dough and turn it out onto a floured surface.
3. Roll out the dough into a rectangle.
4. Spread the date and nut filling evenly over the rolled-out dough.
5. Roll the dough from one long side to form a log.
6. Cut the log into rolls, about 1 to 1.5 inches thick.
7. Place the rolls in the prepared baking dish, leaving space between each.
8. Bake in the preheated oven for 20-25 minutes or until the rolls are golden brown.
9. Allow the Kamut and Date Nut Rolls to cool in the baking dish for a few minutes before transferring them to a wire rack.

These rolls are delicious served warm or at room temperature. The combination of kamut, dates, and nuts creates a flavorful and wholesome treat. Enjoy!

Millet and Sunflower Seed Bagels

Ingredients:

For the Bagels:

- 1 1/2 cups warm water (about 110°F or 43°C)
- 2 tablespoons honey or maple syrup
- 1 tablespoon active dry yeast
- 4 cups bread flour
- 1 cup millet flour
- 1/2 cup sunflower seeds, plus extra for topping
- 1 1/2 teaspoons salt

For Boiling:

- 2 quarts water
- 1 tablespoon honey or barley malt syrup

Instructions:

In a small bowl, combine warm water, honey (or maple syrup), and active dry yeast. Let it sit for 5-10 minutes until frothy.

In a large mixing bowl, combine bread flour, millet flour, sunflower seeds, and salt.

Make a well in the center of the dry ingredients and pour in the yeast mixture. Mix until a dough forms.

Turn the dough onto a floured surface and knead for about 10 minutes until smooth and elastic. Add more flour if necessary.

Place the dough in a lightly oiled bowl, cover it with a damp cloth, and let it rise in a warm place for about 1-1.5 hours, or until doubled in size.

Preheat your oven to 425°F (220°C). Bring 2 quarts of water and honey (or barley malt syrup) to a boil in a large pot.

Punch down the risen dough and divide it into 10-12 equal portions. Shape each portion into a ball.

Flatten each ball and poke a hole through the center, stretching it to form a bagel shape.

Carefully drop the bagels into the boiling water, a few at a time, and boil for 1-2 minutes per side.

Remove the boiled bagels with a slotted spoon and place them on a parchment-lined baking sheet.

Sprinkle the tops of the bagels with additional sunflower seeds.

Bake in the preheated oven for 15-20 minutes or until the bagels are golden brown.

Allow the Millet and Sunflower Seed Bagels to cool on a wire rack before slicing and enjoying.

These bagels are wonderful with your favorite spreads, such as cream cheese, jam, or butter. The addition of millet and sunflower seeds adds a delightful crunch and nutty flavor.

Quinoa and Cranberry Swirl Bread

Ingredients:

For the Dough:

- 1 cup cooked quinoa, cooled
- 1 cup warm milk (about 110°F or 43°C)
- 2 tablespoons honey or maple syrup
- 2 1/4 teaspoons active dry yeast
- 3 1/2 cups all-purpose flour
- 1 teaspoon salt
- 2 tablespoons olive oil or melted butter

For the Filling:

- 1/2 cup dried cranberries
- 1/4 cup honey or maple syrup
- 1 teaspoon ground cinnamon

For Glaze (optional):

- 1/2 cup powdered sugar
- 1-2 tablespoons milk
- 1/2 teaspoon vanilla extract

Instructions:

In a small bowl, combine warm milk, honey (or maple syrup), and active dry yeast. Let it sit for 5-10 minutes until frothy.
In a large mixing bowl, combine all-purpose flour and salt.
Add the cooked quinoa to the flour mixture.
Make a well in the center of the dry ingredients and pour in the yeast mixture and olive oil (or melted butter). Mix until a dough forms.
Turn the dough onto a floured surface and knead for about 8-10 minutes until smooth and elastic. Add more flour if necessary.

Place the dough in a lightly oiled bowl, cover it with a damp cloth, and let it rise in a warm place for about 1-1.5 hours, or until doubled in size.

In a small bowl, mix together dried cranberries, honey (or maple syrup), and ground cinnamon to create the filling.

Preheat your oven to 350°F (175°C). Grease and flour a standard-sized loaf pan.

Punch down the risen dough and roll it out on a floured surface into a rectangle. Spread the cranberry filling evenly over the rolled-out dough.

Roll the dough tightly from one end to form a log. Place the log seam-side down in the prepared loaf pan.

Cover the pan with a damp cloth and let the dough rise for an additional 30-45 minutes.

Bake in the preheated oven for 30-35 minutes or until the bread is golden brown and sounds hollow when tapped on the bottom.

If desired, prepare the glaze by whisking together powdered sugar, milk, and vanilla extract. Drizzle over the cooled bread.

Allow the Quinoa and Cranberry Swirl Bread to cool in the pan for 10 minutes before transferring it to a wire rack to cool completely.

Slice and enjoy this delicious and nutritious bread with the unique combination of quinoa and cranberries!

Whole Wheat Pizza Dough

Ingredients:

- 1 1/2 cups warm water (about 110°F or 43°C)
- 2 1/4 teaspoons active dry yeast
- 1 tablespoon honey or maple syrup
- 3 1/2 cups whole wheat flour
- 2 tablespoons olive oil
- 1 teaspoon salt

Instructions:

In a small bowl, combine warm water, honey (or maple syrup), and active dry yeast. Let it sit for about 5-10 minutes until frothy.
In a large mixing bowl, combine whole wheat flour and salt.
Make a well in the center of the dry ingredients and pour in the yeast mixture and olive oil. Mix until a dough forms.
Turn the dough onto a floured surface and knead for about 8-10 minutes, or until it becomes smooth and elastic. Add more flour if necessary.
Place the dough in a lightly oiled bowl, cover it with a damp cloth, and let it rise in a warm place for about 1-1.5 hours, or until doubled in size.
Preheat your oven to the highest setting (usually around 475°F or 245°C).
Punch down the risen dough and divide it in half for two medium-sized pizzas or keep it as a whole for a larger pizza.
Roll out the dough on a floured surface to your desired thickness.
Transfer the rolled-out dough to a pizza stone or a baking sheet lined with parchment paper.
Add your favorite pizza sauce, cheese, and toppings.
Bake in the preheated oven for 12-15 minutes or until the crust is golden brown and the cheese is melted and bubbly.
Remove from the oven, slice, and enjoy your whole wheat pizza!

Feel free to experiment with toppings and sauces to suit your taste. This whole wheat pizza dough offers a nutty flavor and a hearty texture, making it a healthier alternative to traditional pizza crust.

Buckwheat and Fig Sourdough

Ingredients:

Levain:

- 50 grams mature sourdough starter
- 50 grams whole wheat flour
- 50 grams bread flour
- 100 grams water

Dough:

- 350 grams bread flour
- 100 grams buckwheat flour
- 275 grams water
- 9 grams salt
- 150 grams dried figs, chopped
- Additional water, if needed

Instructions:

Levain:

In a bowl, mix the mature sourdough starter with whole wheat flour, bread flour, and water. Cover and let it ferment at room temperature for 8-12 hours or until doubled in size.

Dough:

In a large mixing bowl, combine the bread flour, buckwheat flour, and water. Mix until a shaggy dough forms. Cover and let it rest for 30-60 minutes (autolyse). Sprinkle the salt over the dough, add the levain, and incorporate them using the "stretch and fold" technique until well combined. Cover and let it rest for 30 minutes.
Perform a series of stretch and folds every 30 minutes for the first 2 hours. After the initial folds, gently incorporate the chopped dried figs into the dough. Continue with a few more stretch and folds, ensuring the figs are evenly distributed.

Cover the bowl and let the dough bulk ferment for an additional 4-6 hours or until it has increased in volume and has a lively, aerated feel.

Pre-shape the dough into a round and let it rest for 20-30 minutes.

Shape the dough into its final shape, place it in a well-floured proofing basket, cover, and refrigerate overnight (or for at least 8 hours).

Preheat your oven to 450°F (232°C). Place a Dutch oven in the oven to preheat. Once the oven is ready, carefully transfer the dough from the proofing basket to the hot Dutch oven. Score the top of the dough with a sharp knife.

Cover the Dutch oven with its lid and bake for 20 minutes. Remove the lid and bake for an additional 20-25 minutes or until the bread has a deep golden brown crust.

Allow the Buckwheat and Fig Sourdough to cool on a wire rack before slicing.

Enjoy the unique combination of nutty buckwheat and sweet figs in this flavorful sourdough bread!

Pumpkin Seed and Apricot Loaf

Ingredients:

- 1 cup warm water (about 110°F or 43°C)
- 2 1/4 teaspoons active dry yeast
- 1 tablespoon honey or maple syrup
- 3 cups bread flour
- 1 cup whole wheat flour
- 1/2 cup pumpkin seeds, plus extra for topping
- 1/2 cup dried apricots, chopped
- 1 teaspoon salt
- 2 tablespoons olive oil or melted butter

Instructions:

In a small bowl, combine warm water, honey (or maple syrup), and active dry yeast. Let it sit for about 5-10 minutes until frothy.

In a large mixing bowl, combine bread flour, whole wheat flour, pumpkin seeds, and salt.

Make a well in the center of the dry ingredients and pour in the yeast mixture and olive oil (or melted butter). Mix until a dough forms.

Turn the dough onto a floured surface and knead for about 8-10 minutes, or until it becomes smooth and elastic. Add more flour if necessary.

Place the dough in a lightly oiled bowl, cover it with a damp cloth, and let it rise in a warm place for about 1-1.5 hours, or until doubled in size.

Preheat your oven to 375°F (190°C). Grease and flour a standard-sized loaf pan.

Punch down the risen dough and turn it out onto a floured surface.

Flatten the dough and sprinkle the chopped dried apricots evenly over it. Fold the dough over and knead it briefly to distribute the apricots.

Shape the dough into a loaf and place it in the prepared loaf pan. Optionally, sprinkle additional pumpkin seeds on top.

Cover the pan with a damp cloth and let the dough rise for an additional 30-45 minutes.

Bake in the preheated oven for 30-40 minutes or until the bread is golden brown and sounds hollow when tapped on the bottom.

Allow the Pumpkin Seed and Apricot Loaf to cool in the pan for 10 minutes before transferring it to a wire rack to cool completely.

Slice and enjoy this flavorful and nutritious loaf with the delightful combination of pumpkin seeds and apricots!

Teff and Date Flatbread

Ingredients:

- 1 cup teff flour
- 1/2 cup all-purpose flour
- 1 teaspoon baking powder
- 1/2 teaspoon salt
- 1 cup water
- 1 tablespoon olive oil
- 1/2 cup chopped dates

Instructions:

In a mixing bowl, combine teff flour, all-purpose flour, baking powder, and salt. Gradually add water and olive oil to the dry ingredients, stirring continuously to avoid lumps. Mix until you achieve a smooth batter.
Fold in the chopped dates into the batter, ensuring they are evenly distributed.
Heat a non-stick skillet or griddle over medium heat.
Pour a ladleful of the batter onto the hot skillet, spreading it out into a round shape.
Cook the flatbread for 2-3 minutes on each side, or until golden brown and cooked through.
Repeat the process with the remaining batter, adjusting the heat if necessary.
Once cooked, transfer the Teff and Date Flatbreads to a plate.
Serve warm and enjoy!

This flatbread is a delightful combination of the earthy flavor of teff and the natural sweetness of dates. It's perfect as a side dish, for dipping into sauces, or as a base for various toppings. Experiment with different herbs or spices to customize the flavor to your liking.

Amaranth and Currant Bread

Ingredients:

- 1 cup amaranth flour
- 2 cups all-purpose flour
- 1 packet (2 1/4 teaspoons) active dry yeast
- 1 teaspoon salt
- 1 tablespoon honey or maple syrup
- 1 cup warm water (about 110°F or 43°C)
- 2 tablespoons olive oil
- 1/2 cup dried currants

Instructions:

In a small bowl, combine warm water, honey (or maple syrup), and active dry yeast. Allow it to sit for about 5-10 minutes, or until it becomes frothy.
In a large mixing bowl, combine amaranth flour, all-purpose flour, and salt.
Make a well in the center of the dry ingredients and pour in the yeast mixture and olive oil. Mix until a dough forms.
Turn the dough onto a floured surface and knead for about 8-10 minutes, or until it becomes smooth and elastic. Add more flour if necessary.
Place the dough in a lightly oiled bowl, cover it with a damp cloth, and let it rise in a warm place for about 1-1.5 hours, or until it has doubled in size.
Preheat your oven to 375°F (190°C). Grease or line a baking sheet.
Punch down the risen dough and turn it out onto a floured surface.
Flatten the dough and sprinkle the dried currants evenly over it. Fold the dough over and knead it briefly to distribute the currants.
Shape the dough into a round or oval loaf and place it on the prepared baking sheet.
Optionally, slash the top of the loaf with a sharp knife to allow for expansion during baking.
Bake in the preheated oven for 30-40 minutes or until the bread is golden brown and sounds hollow when tapped on the bottom.
Allow the Amaranth and Currant Bread to cool on a wire rack before slicing and serving.

This bread is perfect for breakfast or as a snack. The combination of amaranth and currants adds a unique and delightful flavor to the bread. Enjoy!

Sunflower Seed and Honey Rye Bread

Ingredients:

- 1 1/2 cups warm water (about 110°F or 43°C)
- 2 1/4 teaspoons active dry yeast
- 2 tablespoons honey
- 1 cup rye flour
- 2 1/2 cups bread flour
- 1/4 cup olive oil or melted butter
- 1 teaspoon salt
- 1/2 cup sunflower seeds (plus extra for topping)
- Additional honey for brushing (optional)

Instructions:

In a small bowl, combine warm water, honey, and active dry yeast. Allow it to sit for about 5-10 minutes or until frothy.

In a large mixing bowl, combine rye flour, bread flour, and salt.

Make a well in the center of the dry ingredients and pour in the yeast mixture and olive oil (or melted butter). Mix until a dough forms.

Turn the dough onto a floured surface and knead for about 8-10 minutes, or until it becomes smooth and elastic. Add more flour if necessary.

Place the dough in a lightly oiled bowl, cover it with a damp cloth, and let it rise in a warm place for about 1-1.5 hours, or until it has doubled in size.

Preheat your oven to 375°F (190°C). Grease or line a baking sheet.

Punch down the risen dough and turn it out onto a floured surface.

Flatten the dough and sprinkle sunflower seeds evenly over it. Fold the dough over and knead it briefly to distribute the sunflower seeds.

Shape the dough into a round or oval loaf and place it on the prepared baking sheet.

Optionally, brush the top of the loaf with honey and sprinkle additional sunflower seeds on top.

Bake in the preheated oven for 30-40 minutes or until the bread is golden brown and sounds hollow when tapped on the bottom.

Allow the Sunflower Seed and Honey Rye Bread to cool on a wire rack before slicing and serving.

This bread has a rich, nutty flavor from the combination of rye flour and sunflower seeds, complemented by the sweetness of honey. It's perfect for sandwiches or enjoyed on its own.

www.ingramcontent.com/pod-product-compliance
Lightning Source LLC
LaVergne TN
LVHW061944070526
838199LV00060B/3960